"Psychologist Jay Earley shows hov
the Perfectionism pattern, which can be so self-destructive.
He explores the motivations behind different varieties of
perfectionism and provides healing practices for developing
more ease and perspective in our lives. This restores a more
balanced and serene view of ourselves and makes our daily
actions more fulfilling for ourselves and others. But even
more, this special kind of ebook offers the reader continuous
technological assistance to systematically engage in the healing
practice in your life. And even more, as an option, you can join
an online community to share the journey. A great value for
anyone serious in wanting to stop the battle with yourself and
start to enjoy your life!"

— Jean-Pierre Marceau D.Ps., Psychologist

"Like Earley's other publications, I really enjoyed reading this
book as it was not full of 'jargon' and it really allowed me to zone
in on the issues most relevant to me. I gained so much from the
questionnaire as well as the stories about people I could relate to.
This book contains helpful tools that I can read and refer back to,
to begin to find freedom from the need to act perfect all the time.
I have already recommended it to a couple of friends. I imagine it
will be an eye-opening experience for those who, like me, had no
idea that they were in a prison of perfectionism."

— Danielle L. Owen, LADCII, Substance Abuse Counselor

"As expected, Jay Earley's latest book, *Letting Go of Perfectionism*,
is written in a very clear and accessible style for both the
professional and general reader. As a psychologist who is a big
fan of IFS, I find the comprehensive scope of Earley's *Pattern
System* very useful for deepening my understanding of the
psyche and how wounds from early childhood set the tone
for challenges in later life. It has especially helped me to get
acquainted with my 'inner critics' and get them to work for me
instead of undermining my every move. I am also struck with
the cutting-edge nature of the Kindle format linked with an
online workbook. The use of practice notes and daily check-in
notes helped me to log my personal struggle with my inner
critics in real time and put my insights into immediate action
to promote insight and healing."

— Tom Burdenski, PhD, Licensed Psychologist,
Associate Professor of Psychology and Counseling

Letting Go of Perfectionism

Gaining Perspective, Balance, and Ease

Jay Earley, PhD and Bonnie Weiss, LCSW

 PATTERN SYSTEM BOOKS
Larkspur, CA

LETTING GO OF PERFECTIONISM:
Gaining Perspective, Balance, and Ease

▧ PATTERN SYSTEM BOOKS

140 Marina Vista Ave.
Larkspur, CA 94939
415-924-5256
www.patternsystembooks.com

Paperback ISBN-13: 978-0-9855937-4-2
LCCN: 2012911093

Printed in the United States of America

Introduction to the
Inner Critic Series

Because the Inner Critic is one of the most challenging issues people face, we have engaged in a multiyear study and practice on how to transform the Critic. We have identified seven types of Inner Critics (see Appendix B) and have learned how to work most effectively with each one. We have also pioneered the concept of the Inner Champion as an antidote to the Inner Critic. This work is spelled out in our book *Self-Therapy for Your Inner Critic.*

While the first book in the series focused on all seven Critics, this book and each of the others focuses on one of the seven, showing how to work with and transform it.

These book are also based on the *Pattern System*SM—a comprehensive mapping of the human psyche developed by Jay. You can use the Pattern System to obtain a complete map of your psyche. You will be able to see your strengths and your defenses, your places of pain and how you compensate for them. You'll come to understand the structure of your inner conflicts and see where you are ready to grow. The Pattern System makes clear what you need to explore next in order to resolve the issues that are most important to you.

You'll learn where there is underlying pain, shame, or fear that must be healed. You'll also learn which healthy psychological capacities you can develop (or are already developing) to become happier and more productive.

In the Pattern System, *patterns* represent dysfunctional behaviors that cause problems for us or other people. *Healthy capacities* are the ways we feel and act that make our lives productive, connected, and happy. The Pattern System organizes the patterns and capacities according to various psychological *dimensions,* such as intimacy, power, and self-esteem. See http://thepatternsystem.wikispaces.com for an outline and more complete description of the Pattern System.

Each one of the seven Critics corresponds to a pattern in the Pattern System, so each book in the series shows how to work with this pattern and break free from it. In the process of learning about each pattern, you can delve into its *motivations* and the *wounds* behind them. This will help you to transform your way of living from the pattern to its corresponding healthy capacity. This book also shows you how to transform the particular Critic and activate the Inner Champion so you are free of attacks from the Critic and can live from the healthy capacity.

Acknowledgments

We are grateful for detailed and helpful suggestions from Anna Rosenhauer, Joseph Luther, Krissy Tingle, Dorothea Hrossowyc, Tom Burdenski, Jean-Pierre Marceau, Roger Desmarais, Everett Considine, and Danielle Owen.

We appreciate the sharp eyes and clear mind of Kira Freed, who provided quality editing. Kira also did excellent work on the interior design for the paperback version. As always, we love the clear aesthetic that Jeannene Langford brings to cover design.

Kathy Wilber is a joy to work with and has done an excellent job on the programming behind the workbook. Our virtual assistant, Doreen DeJesus, has been continually in the background, helping with many tasks that keep our work flowing.

Contents

Introduction

Do you feel that the work you produce is never good enough? Do you work endlessly on projects or run them right up to the deadline? Is it hard for you to even start on a project because you fear it won't be good enough? Do you sit staring at your computer, unable to get going? Do you feel that your appearance, your home, or your children must be perfect or else you are a failure? Do you believe that making a mistake is the worst thing you can do?

If you answered yes to some of these questions, you may be one of the many people suffering from Perfectionism. If so, you have a need to be perfect that goes far beyond what is actually required for excellence. This overblown demand on yourself can get in the way of your getting jobs done on time because you spend far too much time on them. Alternatively, it can lead you to procrastinate and avoid working on projects.

Perfectionism can cause you to be uptight and worried much of the time. It can keep you from being relaxed and having fun and joy in life. It can unbalance your life because you spend far too much time on work or other attempts to be perfect, leaving little time for family, friends, love, and creativity.

This book can help you let go of this exaggerated need to be perfect. It will help you be more present in each moment and less attached to outcomes. You'll be able to complete your work without forcing it to be perfect, instead noticing when it feels "good enough" and allowing it to come to a natural completion. The book will help you do your work in a way that flows so you can feel more pleasure and lightness. You'll go through your life in a more relaxed way, without pushing, yet still making progress with your work. You'll be able to take time for your other needs, such as socializing, relaxation, fun, and personal health.

We invite you to read this book and do the exercises so you can gain perspective on what is needed and be at ease as you produce excellent work while having a balanced, relaxed, and happy life.

The Pattern System and Internal Family Systems Therapy

This book is primarily based on the Pattern System (see Introduction to the Inner Critic Series). Internal Family Systems Therapy (IFS) is an extremely powerful and user-friendly form of psychotherapy that we use and teach. IFS and the Pattern System complement each other. The Pattern

System provides a theory of the psychological content of the human psyche, while IFS provides a powerful method for healing and transformation of psychological problems.

We have chosen to write this book in such a way that you don't need to understand anything about IFS or parts. For those of you who already know IFS, the concepts in this book are completely compatible with it and can enhance your IFS work on yourself. In Chapter 9, we explain how IFS can be helpful in enhancing the work described in this book.

How to Use This Book

You can use this book to explore either your own Perfectionist Pattern or that of another person. The book is written in terms of the reader's pattern, but you can easily apply what you learn to other people. Gaining an understanding of Perfectionism can aid you in having compassion for and interacting with someone with that pattern. Chapter 2 is for those of you who are reading this specifically to learn about another person.

Visit http://www.personal-growth-programs.com/letting-go-of-perfectionism-owners to register yourself as an owner of this book, and I will immediately send you an ebook version.[1] As we write subsequent books in this series, we keep noticing improvements we want to make in previous books. If you register as an owner of this book, every time we improve the book, we will email you the latest ebook version. You will also be notified about each new book in the series as it comes out.

---

1. I will send you a Kindle version, which you can read on your computer, tablet, or smartphone using free software that you can download from Amazon.

Even though this book is a workbook, there is also a
workbook on the web at http://www.personalgrowth
application.com/Pattern/PerfectionistPatternWorkbook/
Perfectionist_Pattern_Workbook.aspx that goes with this
book. There are many places in the book where you can
check off items or fill in blanks. You have a choice of doing this directly in this book or using the web workbook instead. All the information in the web workbook will be held
under your name and password with complete confidenti-
ality and security. At any point, you will be able to return to
the web workbook to look at your answers, change them, or
print them out. You will be able to use either workbook to
engage in the life practice in Chapter 7.

This book is aimed at helping you change. Therefore, it is
crucial that you fill out the Workbook and do the practice to
have more ease in your life.

We are forming an Online Community of people who are
reading this book and would like to support each other in
letting go of Perfectionism. You can find the Online Community at http://www.personal-growth-programs.com/
connect. We will help you find a buddy to talk with as you
are reading the book, and especially as you are engaging in
the life practice in Chapter 7. You can participate in discussions and phone meetings where you share your struggles
and triumphs with others who are dealing with the same
issues around Perfectionism. The calls and discussions will
be facilitated by one of us or a colleague, and we will be
available to answer your questions.

This support could make all the difference in your success at using this book to let go of Perfectionism. It is part
of a larger community of people who are working on per-

sonal growth and healing through our books, websites, and programs.

Many different patterns are mentioned at various points in this book. Most of these are just for you to explore in more detail if you choose to. If you only want to move ahead to get help with your Perfectionist Pattern, feel free to ignore these patterns. It isn't important that you remember or understand them. Just keep reading to get the help you want.

We congratulate you on your willingness to embark on this exciting inner journey. You will soon discover how the Perfectionist Pattern operates, the unconscious motives behind it, and where they likely came from in your childhood. You will discover how to transform this pattern and the Perfectionist Inner Critic. You will also explore the various aspects of the Ease Capacity and how to cultivate them. And finally, you will have the opportunity to gain ease and balance in your life while producing excellent work.

CHAPTER 1

Your Perfectionist Pattern

If you have the Perfectionist Pattern, you try to do everything perfectly. You have extremely high standards for your behavior and especially for any products you create or performances you are tasked to do. With this pattern, you may find that impending writing projects, reports, papers, or presentations cause you a great deal of anxiety because you are so concerned about completing them perfectly. You may consistently feel that your work isn't good enough and that it must be improved before anyone else sees it.

With this pattern, you may doubt the quality of what you have produced by focusing only on its possible shortcomings. By focusing only on your shortcomings, the Perfectionist convinces you that your work isn't good enough and must be improved before anyone sees it. The Perfectionist doesn't want you to run the risk of appearing mediocre or even less than fabulous; you must be perfect and flawless— a "ten"—to pass the gate. The result might be that you end up working much harder and longer on a project than is really necessary.

Of course, there may be a few situations in which you *need* to be perfect, or nearly so, for example, if you are proofreading or competing in gymnastics. But if you find yourself trying to be perfect much of the time or when it isn't really needed, this indicates a Perfectionist Pattern.

If you have the Perfectionist Pattern strongly, you may find you often are unable to turn anything in until you have reached the absolute deadline, or you may consistently turn in work late. You're likely to be afraid to finish a project because then you run the risk of exposing your shortcomings and being judged or, worse, ridiculed.

If your Perfectionist Pattern includes self-judgment about not being perfect, then it is also a Perfectionist Inner Critic. An Inner Critic is a part that judges us and makes us feel bad about ourselves. There are a number of flavors of Inner Critics.[2]

The Perfectionist Inner Critic is a part of you, reminiscent of a disapproving parent or teacher, that judges you harshly, saying that your efforts are "stupid," "lazy," or "sloppy." You hold these beliefs regardless of what other people say

2. We have identified seven types of Inner Critics, of which the Perfectionist is one. We have written about how to work with these parts and transform them in *Self-Therapy for Your Inner Critic* and *Activating Your Inner Champion Instead of Your Inner Critic.*

to the contrary. You might also have difficulty accepting others' praise of your work. Your Perfectionist Critic will focus entirely on what isn't perfect and fail to appreciate what you have done well.

A Perfectionist Pattern can also show up in concern over your appearance. You may believe you must be impeccably groomed and behave with perfect etiquette in all situations. You might strive to keep a flawlessly clean and beautiful house, and even to have a perfect family. With a strong Perfectionist Pattern, you may strain to make perfect choices in every situation, believing any kind of mistake is unspeakable failure.

Each pattern contains a false belief that gets the person in trouble. Here is the one for the Perfectionist Pattern: "You must be perfect every time. Anything other than absolute perfection is unacceptable."

People can have many possible dynamics around Perfectionism. In this book, we will lay out the various ways that you might strive to be perfect and why, so you can understand your patterns and change them.

A Story of a Perfectionist Pattern

Stories have always been an excellent learning tool. Oftentimes it is easier to get glimpses of yourself in another person's story.

Jeremy was always smart as a whip. As soon as you spent some time with him, it was clear. And if you hung around a little longer, you'd see that he was creative, artistic, and easily thought out of the box. Sounds like a ticket to success, right? Not quite.

Jeremy's Midwestern family did not support his capacities. He wasn't a toiler but was inclined to hop to the end of a project because he didn't want to finish what wasn't a challenge. His father was always strict and critical, and very often deeply disappointed in Jeremy, as he was with his own life. They clashed over and over.

Jeremy moved away from home and began to get some better opportunities for success, based on his apparent talents. He wanted to please his bosses in Silicon Valley and prove how skilled he really was. He would take on a project and overpromise his deadline, when deep inside he knew it was an impossible task. He usually almost finished the job on time.

Unfortunately, his Perfectionist kicked in, saying it knew he could do better. He would work all night trying to make things perfect. This would lead to his coming in late or not showing up at work. His bosses thought he was lazy and not taking the job seriously. He was too afraid to ask for help or even give his superiors realistic progress reports. He worried that doing this would make him seem deficient. So he fell further and further behind and lost opportunity after opportunity. This, of course, angered everyone around him.

At the age of twenty-three, he was against a wall: enormous talent, a good deal of accumulated experience, but his work grinding to halt. It was clear that Jeremy needed to make some peace with his Perfectionism and take back control of his life. When he studied the Pattern System, he started to understand more about his Perfectionist Pattern and what kept it in place. Jeremy's story will be continued in Chapter 3.

Perfectionist Behaviors and Feelings

The following are common behaviors and feelings that come from the Perfectionist Pattern. Which of these apply to you?

- ☐ I have a hard time finishing projects because I always feel they could be better.
- ☐ I believe there's a "right" way to do things.
- ☐ I judge myself harshly for mistakes.
- ☐ It's hard for me to start producing things because I feel that they won't be good enough.
- ☐ I believe my appearance must be impeccable.
- ☐ I focus on what isn't perfect and obsess about it.
- ☐ I have a hard time receiving compliments for things I do because I don't think they are good enough.
- ☐ I judge myself as lazy or sloppy if I don't handle every conceivable issue perfectly.

- ☐ Other behavior _____

      _____

- ☐ Other feelings _____

      _____

If you prefer to use a workbook on the web rather than filling out your answers in this book or on paper, visit http://www.personalgrowthapplication.com/Pattern/Perfectionist PatternWorkbook/Perfectionist_Pattern_Workbook_Behaviors_and_Thoughts.aspx.

You don't have to engage in all these behaviors to have the Perfectionist Pattern. And for the ones you do have, you don't have to be doing them all the time.

Your Perfectionist Pattern might be operating all the time, or it might be triggered only under certain circumstances, such as when you have an important work project to complete or when you're getting dressed for an important social function. Think about the circumstances that tend to trigger your Perfectionism.

Perfectionist Thoughts

If you listen carefully to your thoughts, you may become aware of ones that are related to Perfectionism. Here are some examples. Which ones resonate with you, and in which situations do they tend to come up?

- ❐ That's not good enough.
- ❐ You could do better than that. It has to be perfect.
- ❐ That is not acceptable.
- ❐ You should be able to do it perfectly the first time.

❐ Don't even try unless it's going to be of superior quality.

❐ They expect better from you.

❐ There is one right way, and you have to follow it.

❐ You're not done until it's perfect.

❐ You can't do anything right.

❐ Keep trying until it's perfect.

❐ You do such a slipshod job.

❐ Don't settle for less than perfect.

❐ You and yours should always seem perfect.

❐ What a mess! You are out of control.

❐ Everyone and everything has to be a certain way.

❐ Other behavior _____

_____

❐ Other feelings _____

_____

Situations that Trigger Perfectionism

What are typical situations that trigger your Perfectionist Pattern—for example projects, tests, your appearance, your home, dangerous circumstances? List the situations in which you become perfectionistic. Be very specific—for example, proposals for work, talks at conferences, papers for homework, your children's behavior. You will process them later in the book.

_____

_____

_____

_____

_____

Types of Perfectionist Patterns

There are a number of different kinds of Perfectionist Patterns. Check off the ones that are closest to yours.

❑ Not Enough

You always believe that you must do more on projects because they are not good enough yet. You work far too long on tasks because you are never satisfied that they are OK. You often work right up until deadlines and often turn your work in late. You don't want to officially finish projects because then you run the risk of exposing your shortcomings and being judged, and—even worse—ridiculed.

❐ Creative Block

You can't produce anything because it has to be perfect the first time. Your ideas are blocked because they aren't good enough to put out. Your Perfectionist Critic doesn't allow you to be a learner or to experiment because both of those situations involve putting out work that is far from perfect at first.

For example, Sarah suffered from writer's block. She would sit down to work on a paper, come up with an idea to get started, and then say, "That is such a dumb idea. Don't even bother!" Or she would say, "I'd better write this really well or I'll really be shamed when my teacher sees it." As a result, she wouldn't be able to get started on the paper. She would just sit there trying to write, and nothing would come. She was so afraid of being judged and rejected that she wouldn't let herself produce anything. She didn't realize that most people start out with writing that isn't that good and then improve it.

❐ Control

Your world must be perfectly in control and in order. You must get everything right. You must always do the right thing and make the right choice. Your home and family must look perfect. You must be perfectly groomed and behave impeccably. You exert rigid control over your behavior, which takes away your vitality and spontaneity. Your life must be perfectly in control and predictable in order for you to feel safe.[3]

---

3. This is related to the Controlling Pattern (http://personal-growth-pro grams.com/controlling-pattern). Follow these links (and those throughout the rest of the book) to see if the books for these patterns are now available.

❑ Inner Critic

In order to enforce the goal of being perfect, your Perfectionist Inner Critic judges you or shames you about your work or your life whenever it feels that you aren't living up to its expectations. It tells you that you are stupid, incompetent, sloppy, inappropriate, bad, and so on. You may end up feeling worthless, depressed, or inadequate. This type may be combined with any of the others.

Note that it is possible to have any (or all) of the first three types of Perfectionism without an Inner Critic if you strive to be perfect in those ways. The Inner Critic comes in as an enforcer when you aren't striving hard enough for perfection. Its attacks are aimed at making you try harder to be perfect.

If you would like to take a quiz to help you determine which of these sub-patterns you have, visit http://www. personalgrowthapplication.com/Members/Questionnaire. aspx?Questionnaire=10.

Notice that some of these types are related to other patterns, which you might need to explore to work through your Perfectionism. Click on the links in the footnotes to see which of those books are available now.

Please don't feel that you have to remember all the different patterns and capacities that are introduced in this book. Just explore the ones that are relevant for you. The Pattern System will gradually make sense the more you use it. To see an overview of the whole system, read Appendix A or visit http://thepatternsystem.wikispaces.com.

As you read about these patterns that you might have (and others later in the book), please don't judge yourself because you may have some of them. We all have a variety of different patterns of relating that don't work for us. There is nothing deficient or wrong with you because you have some—in fact, just the opposite. You are reading this book because you are interested in learning about yourself and changing your patterns. You are to be congratulated for your commitment to self-awareness.

At this point, if you aren't sure whether you have the Perfectionist Pattern or another pattern related to accomplishment, read Chapter 8 and take the quiz on the Accomplishment Dimension. Then if you do have the Perfectionist Pattern, return and continue with Chapter 2.

Other People's Patterns

This chapter contains a lot of material condensed into a short space. Take your time reading and reflecting on what is here.

How Your Perfectionist Pattern May Affect
Your Perception of Other People

When you are coming from your Perfectionist Pattern, you might think that another person has a Sloppy Pattern even if he or she doesn't. Someone might appear sloppy to you because of your demand for perfection even if they are doing a decent job.

When Your Perfectionist Is Directed
Toward Other People

So far we have been discussing situations in which your Perfectionist Critic directs its demands and judgment toward you. However, sometimes this part will turn its attention outward and try to make other people perfect. In this case, you may see others as sloppy, stupid, or incompetent. You may enjoy correcting them about small things, even when they haven't asked for your feedback. You may be demanding and picky in what you expect from others. You may apply your very high standards to other people's products, appearance, or behavior and be dissatisfied with anything less.[4]

This can hurt other people and cause them to get angry at you or withdraw from you. If you are close to someone who tends to be more on the loose and sloppy side, this can cause arguments between you and possibly create big problems in your relationship.

If Someone Close to You Is a Perfectionist

If you suspect that someone close to you has a Perfectionist Pattern, you're probably reading this book to try and understand his or her behavior and feelings. This can be very helpful in getting clear on where this person is coming from.

In addition, this book can help you understand yourself more deeply. It is possible that you are inadvertently contributing to this person's Perfectionism by being perfectionistic toward them—demanding impossible levels of perfor-

---

4. This may be related to your Judgmental Pattern (http://www.personal-growth-programs.com/judgmental-pattern).

mance from them. Consider whether or not this might be the case before trying to help this person.

Another possibility is that someone close to you demands perfection from you or judges you when you fall short. In other words, perhaps this person's Perfectionism is directed toward you. This can be very difficult and painful, and can cause problems in your relationship.

It is possible that you may be contributing to this problem by being too loose or sloppy in the way you do things. In other words, consider whether you are giving this person reason to worry about your not performing well, thereby triggering his or her perfectionist streak. For example, if you tend to leave a mess around the house, your roommate might feel justified in bugging you all the time. Also consider whether you might be unconsciously rebelling against a perfectionist by being very imperfect.

If this might be the case, it would be wise to work on yourself first and improve yourself to the point where you are competent and thorough. Then, if this person still judges you for not being good enough, you can be more sure that it is their issue.

How to Relate to an Inner-Directed Perfectionist

If someone you are close to is perfectionistic with him or herself, try to avoid triggering this person's fears. Read Chapter 3 and Chapter 4 to get a sense of which underlying fears they might have that lead them to be perfectionistic. Talk with this person to get a clearer sense of what they are afraid of. This will help you be aware of times when you unintentionally trigger this person's fears.

For example, if this person is afraid of being judged or

shamed for not being good enough, be on the lookout for anything you might say that contains any hint of criticism. Even if this person is overly sensitive to judgment, you can maximize the chances of their feeling safe with you by watching what you say.

When this person says you are being critical, stop for a moment before you respond. Consider what they are saying. Take them seriously without being defensive. See if you can become aware of your judgmental behavior in the future. You can even make a point of giving this person compliments on the work they produce and the steps they take, no matter how small.

How to Relate to an Outer-Directed Perfectionist

If someone you are close to pushes you to be perfect and judges you when you aren't, this may trigger patterns in you. It might trigger your Angry, Defiant, or Passive-Aggressive Pattern in order to rebel against their demands. It might trigger your Distancing Pattern to get away from them. Do your best to avoid reacting to their Perfectionism. Remember that you are in charge of how you handle your life, and you don't have to meet this person's standards. See if you can stop for a breath rather than reacting in your usual way.

Tell this person that you would like them to allow you to set your own standards unless it involves something that affects them. Ask them to allow you to make your own choices about how you handle your pursuit of excellence. For example, if your spouse is always correcting you about the way you pronounce names, let them know that that is your business, and you aren't concerned about these minor mistakes (if that is the case).

If this person's criticism is related to something that **does** affect them, the two of you will have to talk through the issue to resolve it. For example, if you leave a mess around the house, this may really affect your roommate. Or if the person won't stop judging you, you will have to learn how to work it out with them.

Tell this person about your desire to work through this issue so the two of you aren't at odds about it. Don't bring this up when you are fighting; rather, initiate it when you're in a good place with each other. Sow your seeds in a field that is fertile. Make sure that you aren't coming from a place of resentment. Let this person know how you are affected by their criticism. Do this in a vulnerable way, if possible, for example, by allowing them to see your hurt.

Ask this person if they would be willing to explore the patterns that cause problems in your relationship. Would this person be willing to look at the interactive patterns between you that lead to problems, including whether or not they might have a Perfectionist Pattern? Explain what that means and ask if the person would be interested in reading parts of this book. Would it be better for the person to do this alone or with you? Would it be better for you to explain the ideas to them?

Then ask if this person would like to work with you on changing the relationship for the better. Notice that we are encouraging you to **ask** this person these questions. Give them a chance to say what they believe, want, and are willing to do. See if you can engage them as a willing participant in your quest for greater harmony. Make sure you are bringing this up from an open place.[5]

---

5. You will be more successful at this if you have developed the Good Communication Capacity (http://www.personal-growth-programs. com/blaming-pattern).

CHAPTER 3

The Underlying Motivation for Perfectionism

The next five chapters constitute the heart of the change process for Perfectionism. Here is an outline:

- Chapters 3 & 4: Understand underlying motivations (mainly fears) for Perfectionism and their origins in childhood.

- Chapter 5: Explore the Ease Capacity that you will develop to replace Perfectionism, and work through your fears so your Perfectionism begins to let go.

- Chapter 6: Develop your Ease Inner Champion to counter the attacks of your Perfectionist Inner Critic.

- Chapter 7: Engage in a life practice to create Ease in your life rather than Perfectionism.

Motivations for Perfectionism

In order to change your Perfectionist Pattern, it is very helpful to understand the underlying motivations behind it and its origins in your childhood.

There are many reasons why a pattern like this might develop. Some are outlined here. You may strive for perfection because you are afraid of being emotionally harmed or rejected if you don't measure up. You might also be trying to get acceptance, approval, caring, or love by being perfect.

Or you might be afraid of things getting out of control if you are not perfectly in charge.

Some of your fears might be conscious, but others can be deeply buried. You might even know that there is no real danger if you aren't perfect, but an unconscious part of you is still afraid of it.

This chapter introduces another concept from the Pattern System. *Motivations* are the underlying reasons behind your patterns—what drives them. Your motivations might involve fears, attempts to get love or more self-esteem, or other intentions.

How to Approach This Information

There is potentially painful material to explore in this chapter and the next one. Take it slowly and make sure that you are OK emotionally. Take a break any time you feel the need. You might want to call a friend to talk about the feelings that are coming up, if that would help you feel supported through this process.

As you read through these motivations and think about the ones that pertain to you, please don't judge yourself. It is common for our Inner Critics to use this information to make us feel bad about ourselves. They tell us that we are really screwed up, that we'll never be good enough. Don't believe these self-attacks.

Keep in mind that everyone has a host of fears, needs, and other underlying motivations for their behavior. And everyone has had a variety of childhood wounds. We don't all have the same wounds and fears, but we all have plenty of them. It is perfectly normal to have a variety of these issues.

You aren't bad or pathological or inadequate because of

the ones you have. If your Inner Critic is beating you up about your fears, let it know that judgment isn't helpful. When you can take in new information from an open place, it helps you to see yourself more clearly.

Adopt an attitude of looking at yourself objectively and compassionately as you explore your motivations and wounds. This approach is enormously helpful in learning about yourself. You had to develop these patterns of defense because of the ways you were wounded when you were very young and vulnerable. They aren't your fault. Appreciate yourself for being interested in delving into this material so you can change your Perfectionist Pattern.

Motivations

Let's look at the different motivations for Perfectionism to see which ones resonate with you. Look over the following to see which ones apply to you. If you aren't sure, read the next chapter for more details about each of these motivations and where they come from in childhood.

Fear of Harm

- ☑ I am afraid of being criticized if I am not perfect or if I don't perform perfectly.
- ☑ I am afraid of being shamed if I am not perfect or if I don't perform perfectly.
- ☐ I am afraid of being controlled by someone who feels a need to oversupervise me if I'm not perfect.
- ☑ I am afraid of being yelled at or hit if I am not perfect or if I don't perform perfectly.

Fear of Rejection

☐ I am afraid of being abandoned or of not being cared for or loved if I am not perfect or if I don't perform perfectly.

☑ I am afraid of being rejected if I am not perfect or if I don't perform perfectly.

☐ I am afraid of being dismissed, discounted, and not valued if I'm not perfect or if I don't perform perfectly.

Attempt to Get Connection

☑ I am trying to get acceptance and interest by being perfect so I don't feel unlikable.

☐ I am trying to get approval and admiration by being perfect so I feel good about myself and don't feel deficient.

☐ I am trying to get love by being perfect so I don't feel unlovable.

☐ I am trying to get caring by being perfect so I don't feel deprived and abandoned.

Fear of Disaster

☐ I am afraid that things will get out of control and lead to disaster if I'm not perfect.

Belief in Perfection

☐ I believe it's right to be perfect and wrong to make any mistakes.

Being the Opposite of a Parent

☐ My mother (or father) was so sloppy and flaky that it was embarrassing and made my life difficult, so I swore I would never be like that. I went to the opposite extreme and tried to be perfect in all things.

Jeremy's Motivations

This is a continuation of Jeremy's story from Chapter 1. Once Jeremy started studying the Pattern System, he learned that he had two critics: a Perfectionist and a Taskmaster. They worked in tandem to logjam his capacity to succeed at anything that he attempted. The Taskmaster wanted him to work hard and show the world (mainly his father) that he could achieve success with his skills by working in his own way. It pushed him to keep working and to make promises about what he would deliver without considering the reality. He was able to trace the origins of these patterns in his relationship with his father by studying the Pattern System and exploring his memories of his childhood.

JEREMY: "Nothing I ever did seemed to be good enough for my father. No matter how hard I worked and what I produced, he tore me down and criticized everything I did. I now realize that I assumed I was going to fail regardless of how hard I worked, and I also see now that my father's approval was like a carrot always dangling in front of me—a lure that was always out of reach. Those emotions keep me in a pattern of promising an outrageously high level of performance that I can't ever live up to. They also keep me longing for something from my boss that I really wanted from my father."

The Perfectionist believed that he could always do better and was reluctant to allow him to show anyone any of his work along the way. It chided him and goaded him into redoing things again and again.

JEREMY: "I believe I need to completely 'wow' my boss to earn my keep at work, so I'm always second-guessing my work and trying to figure out how to improve it. I'm afraid of turning in work because I expect to be criticized for it, and some part of me desperately seeks my boss's approval. I see now that I'm trying to avoid being judged as 'less than' by my boss, which would reenact the dynamic with my father."

Today, a part of him still believes that turning in work will make him an easy target for his boss's sharp criticism, so he finds ways to avoid those deadlines altogether.

We will continue with Jeremy's story in Chapter 5.

The next chapter goes into more detail about each of these motivations and their origins in your childhood situation.

CHAPTER 4

Details About Motivations and Childhood Origins

For each type of motivation from the previous chapter, there is a section in this chapter with more detail about that motivation and the childhood situation it comes from.

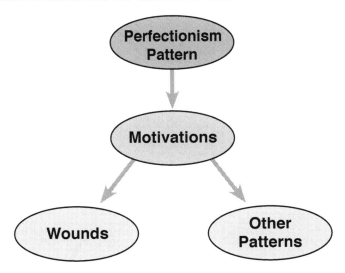

There are a number of different ways to use this chapter.

1. If you already have a pretty good idea about your motivations, you can skip this chapter and perhaps come back to it later to explore where they come from in your childhood.

2. You can go directly to those motivations you checked off in the previous chapter and only explore them.

3. You can read through the entire chapter to get a fuller understanding of your motivations and where they come from. However, if all the detail doesn't feel helpful right now, feel free to skip to the next chapter and come back to this one at a later time.

This chapter introduces another concept from the Pattern System. *Wounds* are the ways you were hurt when you were a child that led to your dysfunctional patterns of behavior as an adult.

How to Approach This Material

Caution: There is a lot of detailed and potentially painful material to explore in this chapter. Feel free to stop at any point when you feel you have processed enough for the moment or for today. Take it slowly and make sure that you are OK emotionally. Take a break any time you feel the need. It often helps to process things gradually. When you sit for a while with something difficult, you can digest it more easily, like a big meal. Call a friend or your buddy from the Perfectionism Online Community to talk about the feelings that are coming up, if that would help you feel supported through this process.

Many motivations and wounds are named in this chapter. It isn't important that you remember or understand them all—only the ones that are relevant to your Perfectionist Pattern. Feel free to ignore the others and just focus on understanding where **your** Perfectionism comes from.

If you have more than one of these motivations and wounds, don't try to process them all at once. Monitor yourself so you can process what you are learning and so you don't get overwhelmed emotionally. Just look at some of them, and come back to the others later.

If two or three of these motivations or wounds seem similar to you, don't worry about teasing them out—just check off all of them. For example, if abandonment and rejection seem similar to you, it is probably because you were both abandoned and rejected. Just check off both of them and then, in Chapter 6, process them together.

Now let's begin with the first motivation.

Fear of Harm

You might be afraid of being harmed in some way (for example, criticized, shamed, yelled at) if you aren't perfect. Of course, it is possible that you have really been harmed, but most likely your concerns are at least partly based on your own underlying issues.

There are four types of harm that usually can pose a threat to the Perfectionist Pattern, and each one is related to a wound. Below is a list of the four. Look them over to see which ones fit your Perfectionist Pattern. You may have more than one of them.

❏ **Fear of Criticism**

You may be afraid of being judged if you aren't perfect.

This is related to the *Deficiency Wound*. When you were a child, you may have been criticized and made to feel inadequate, worthless, or bad about yourself when you didn't measure up to your parents' impossibly high standards. You might be afraid of this happening again if you don't meet such standards.

❏ **Fear of Shame**

You may be afraid of being shamed or ridiculed by people if you aren't perfect.

This is related to the *Shame Wound*. When you were little, you may have been ridiculed, shamed, or embarrassed by parents or others you were close to. You might be afraid of this being repeated in your adult life.

❏ **Fear of Being Controlled**

You may be afraid that if you aren't perfect, you will leave other people room to try to control you.

This is related to the *Powerless Wound*. You may have been dominated and controlled by one of your parents, and they justified it by telling you that you weren't good enough, so they had to take over. You may have hated being in that position, so you don't want to allow anyone the chance to do that again.

❏ **Fear of Attack**

You may be afraid that other people are going to get angry with you, so you try to be perfect in order to protect yourself.

This is related to the *Attack Wound*. When you were little, your parents (or others) may have yelled at you because they said you weren't good enough. They may even have abused you physically. Now you might be frightened of being treated that way again.

Soothing Your Pain

As you read through these descriptions of childhood experiences, painful emotions may come up. It is helpful to soothe yourself when this happens. The best way to do this is to treat each painful emotion as coming from a child part of you—an inner child who was wounded when you were young.

Take a moment to contact this child inside of you. You may see an image of this inner child or feel him or her in your body, or just have a sense of the child. Open your heart to this little being. Be the compassionate, nurturing parent that this wounded inner child needs right now. Listen to his or her pain with caring.

Imagine holding this child in your arms. Let the child know that you are there for him or her. Give this inner child the love he or she needs. And give the child whatever else he or she may need—acceptance, validation, encouragement, support, appreciation, and so on. This will keep you from being overwhelmed by the pain that is coming up, and it may even help to heal that wound in you.

To listen to a guided meditation for nurturing this wounded inner child, visit http://www.personalgrowth application.com/Pattern/PerfectionistPatternWorkbook/ Perfectionist_Pattern_Workbook_Inner_Child_Meditation. aspx.

Fear of Rejection

You might be afraid of being rejected in some way if you aren't perfect. Of course, it is possible that you have really been rejected, but most likely your concerns are at least partly based on your own underlying issues.

There are three major types of rejection in the Pattern System, and each is related to a wound. Look them over to see which one fits your Perfectionist Pattern. You might have more than one.

❐ Fear of Abandonment

You may be afraid of being abandoned if you aren't perfect. Or you might be afraid of not being cared for or loved if you aren't perfect.

This is related to the *Need Wound.* You may not have gotten the love and care that you needed when you were young, and your parents may have said or implied that this was because of your flaws. Or you may have been abandoned by your parents at a time when you really needed them, and they gave you the impression that it was because you weren't good enough. They may even have blamed this on something you did that they judged as inadequate.

❐ Fear of Rejection

You may be afraid of being rejected in some way for not being perfect. Or you might be afraid of revealing who you really are beneath the surface, being exposed as imperfect, and consequently being rejected.

This is related to the *Unlovable Wound.* When you were a child, your parents, siblings, or friends may have rejected or dismissed you or treated you as someone who wasn't of value, and you ended up feeling unlovable. Now you might fear that happening again.

❒ **Fear of Dismissal**

You may be afraid of being dismissed, discounted, and not valued if you aren't perfect.

This is related to the *Deficiency Wound*. When you were a child, things you did may have been dismissed and not valued, which may have made you feel inadequate, worthless, or bad about yourself. You might be afraid of this happening again if your products or actions aren't extremely good.

Attempt to Get Connection

You might be trying to get approval, acceptance, love, or caring by being perfect. Look over the four motivations below to see which one fits your Perfectionist Pattern. You might have more than one.

❒ **Attempt to Get Acceptance**

You may be trying to get acceptance and interest by being perfect in order to attract the attention of people who are important to you so you don't feel unlikable or unacceptable.

This is related to the *Unlovable Wound*. When you were a child, your parents, siblings, or friends may have rejected or dismissed you or treated you as someone who wasn't of value, and you ended up feeling unlovable. Now you might be trying to get the acceptance you never had by being perfect.

❒ **Attempt to Get Approval**

You might be trying to get approval and admiration by being perfect so you feel good about yourself and don't feel deficient.

This is related to the *Deficiency Wound*. When you were a child, you may have been criticized and made to feel inadequate, worthless, or bad about yourself when you didn't measure up to your parents' impossibly high standards. Now you might be trying to get the approval you never had by being perfect.

❐ Attempt to Get Love

You might be trying to get love by being perfect so you don't feel unlovable.

This is related to the *Unlovable Wound,* which is described above.

❐ Attempt to Get Caring

You might be trying to get caring by being perfect so you don't feel deprived and abandoned.

This is related to the *Need Wound.* You may not have gotten the love and care you needed when you were young, and your parents said or implied that this was because of your flaws. Or you may have been abandoned by your parents at a time when you really needed them, and they gave you the impression that it was because you weren't good enough. They may even have blamed this on something you did that they judged as inadequate. Now you might be trying to get this love and caring by being perfect.

Fear of Disaster

You might be trying to create safety by being perfect so you don't feel vulnerable to bad things happening to you.

This is related to the *Fear-of-Disaster Wound.* Harmful, painful, or tragic events may have happened often during your childhood, leading you to be frightened about what might happen next in your current life. You may be trying to gain a measure of control in your life now by being perfect. Another possible origin of this wound is that one of your parents was anxious or frightened about disaster, and you took on their anxiety by osmosis.

Belief in Perfection

You may believe that it is right to be perfect and wrong to make any mistakes. There are five possible origins that could contribute to this belief.

Modeling Origin. One of your parents might have been perfectionistic, so you grew up assuming that that is the way a person should be.

Teaching Origin. Your parents may have told you how important it was to not make mistakes and to be as perfect as possible, so you came to believe that that is the way a person should be.

Reward Origin. Your parents may have rewarded you with praise whenever you were perfect, so you came to believe that that is the way a person should be.

Punishment Origin. Your parents may have punished you for any mistakes you made, so you felt that you had to be perfect in order to be safe.

Shaping Origin. Your need to be perfect may have been shaped by your childhood, which involved a combination of modeling, teaching, punishment, and/or reward.

Opposition to a Parent

Your mother (or father) may have been so sloppy and flaky that it was embarrassing and made your life difficult, so you swore that you would never be like that. You might have gone to the opposite extreme and tried to be perfect in all things.

Next Step

Whew! All of that may have been hard to read. Yet it was necessary in order to come to an understanding of what motivates your Perfectionism and where this tendency comes from in your past. This will be helpful in changing this pattern.

You should now have a pretty good idea of your motivations for Perfectionism. Take your time and get emotional support to process these insights. It can be a lot to take on.

You are now prepared to change your Perfectionist Pattern. This process starts in the next chapter.

CHAPTER 5

The Ease Capacity and Working Through Perfectionist Fears

Now that you have an idea of which of your underlying fears are creating Perfectionism, let's work them through. In order to do that, it will be helpful to understand the Ease Capacity, which contains the wisdom needed to let go of Perfectionism. Ease is the capacity that you will be developing to replace Perfectionism.

Ease means accomplishing tasks in a relaxed, easy way, without stress or striving. Your work flows naturally, and you don't need to aim for perfection. You balance your work with the rest of your life. With the Ease Capacity, you are able to take breaks when you need them instead of driving yourself relentlessly. You are also able to recognize when something is "good enough" to be complete. Ease mean recognizing that there are times to push your work to be the best (such as in a job application, where typos could cost you an interview), but there are also just as many times when it's fine to send out your work even if it isn't perfect or incredibly thorough (such as in daily emails to coworkers).

Ease also means feeling confident about your ability to produce excellent work without stressing yourself out to make it perfect. You know that you are competent, and you trust that even when your work isn't perfect at first (as it rarely is), it will be very good in the end. You can allow yourself to learn new skills and to experiment with new ideas without worrying about how good you are at the beginning because you trust that you will do well over time.

When a situation arises such as performing, working on a paper, or having a social event, your Perfectionist Pattern may become activated. This pattern developed in childhood because you were dealing with a dangerous and harmful situation, for example, being ridiculed when you tried to get attention or being told that your work was never good enough. And unconsciously, you believe that this is going to happen again.

However, your current situation is very different from what happened back then. You are no longer vulnerable and dependent like a child. You are autonomous and are no longer subject to the power of your parents. You have many strengths and capacities now as an adult (and possibly because of previous work you have done on yourself) that you didn't have as a child. For example, you are more grounded and centered. You may be able to assert yourself, be perceptive about interpersonal situations, support yourself financially, and so on. You have already accomplished many things in your life and overcome various obstacles. You are an adult with much greater ability to handle yourself. You probably have friends, maybe a spouse or lover, perhaps a community you belong to, a support group, professionals you can rely on. You have people you can turn to if necessary.

This means that you aren't in danger the way you were as a child, and your mature self is available, which wasn't possible when you were young. Therefore, your Perfectionist responses to situations aren't really necessary any longer because they're reactions to the past.

In this chapter, you can work through the fears that lead to Perfectionism for each particular life situation in which it might get triggered. Choose one specific *life situation* and apply the rest of this chapter to it. Then when you are finished with that situation, if you want, you can come back to this chapter and choose a different situation to process.

Let's explore working through the fears for each of the major types of Perfectionism.

The Not-Enough Perfectionist

Wisdom of the Ease Capacity

The Ease Capacity includes the following insights:

a. Excellence usually doesn't simply mean a lack of mistakes. It is much more than that—creativity, presence, innovation, and so on. There are only a few arenas in which a complete lack of mistakes is of overriding concern. For example, in gymnastics competitions, proofreading, and brain surgery, it is crucial to eliminate mistakes as much as possible. However, in creative dance or creative writing, it is the quality that matters, not how perfect it is.

In addition, some projects require a high level of excellence, and others just need to be good enough for their purpose. This depends on both the nature of the project and your reasons for doing it. For example, Sam has been working on the literature review for his dissertation. His Perfectionist Pattern keeps telling him that he has to keep reading and develop a more complete list of all the published articles in the subject area of his dissertation. However, he has already been working on the lit review for a long time and has an extensive list. He now realizes that it is more important to finish his dissertation, graduate, and get on with a new project that is waiting for him. Having the most perfect literature review is not so important; he needs to move on to other things.

b. Proportion and balance in life are very important for your well-being. This includes the ability to take care of yourself, enjoy life, relax, be with your loved ones, and so on. It also includes having time to spend on a variety other tasks that need attention. If you put all your energy into one project, the rest of your life will suffer.

Keeping in mind the wisdom of the Ease Capacity, let's now look at the life situation for which this wisdom would be helpful.

Working Through the Fears
of the Not-Enough Perfectionist — *I am enough*

The situation that activates this type of Perfectionist involves trying to decide whether to turn in a project or continue to work on it. For example, remember from Chapter 1 that Jeremy had a hard time turning in a job because he was afraid that it wasn't good enough and his boss would really be down on him. When you are in this type of situation, remember that you can handle it and are equipped to make this decision without being extreme about it. In childhood, you were attacked or rejected for not being perfect; for example, Jeremy's father was critical and disappointed in him. However, the situation is quite different now. When you remind yourself of this, you can relax and turn in the project. Or if more work needs to be done on the project, you can do just that much and then be done with it.

There are two related things that the Perfectionist Pattern might be afraid of: (1) Your project isn't good enough, or (2) the person or people who will receive and evaluate your project are harsh, judgmental, or rejecting. It is important to evaluate, from a centered place, whether or not these fears are accurate and realistic. Then you can decide what to do.

Unrealistic Fears

If your fears are unfounded and those receiving your project are reasonable people, there are a number of possibilities:

1. The project is excellent as it is, and that will be recognized.

2. The project is good enough. You won't get any flak, so it is more important to turn your attention to other things.

3. The project isn't good enough yet, but you won't be judged or suffer repercussions for turning it in. They will just tell you it needs more work, and you can keep working on it to improve it.

Therefore, there is no problem with turning it in as it is or asking for feedback about whether more work needs to be done. What do you know about the life situation that makes your fear unrealistic?

_____

_____

_____

_____

In Jeremy's case, his boss was reasonable, and his work was generally excellent, but he wasn't sure how much more needed to be done on a given job. Here's how he solved the problem. He experimented with giving his boss feedback on his work and asking for his input. By doing this, he could determine when a project was good enough to turn in and move on to the next one. Jeremy was gradually able to set more realistic goals for himself at work. He learned that everyone wasn't like his father. His boss could be reasoned with and would support him when Jeremy set realistic goals and kept the boss informed about the status of his work. He began to get excellent reviews from his boss, and his career flourished.

Realistic Fears

Suppose the people evaluating your work **are** harsh and judgmental. Then you will want to make a serious effort to be sure the project meets their standards so as to minimize the chances of being attacked. However, even if you do get judged or shamed, you can handle that. You won't fall apart. You have many more internal and external resources for dealing with this situation than you did as a child.

Devise a plan[6] for how you will respond if your work receives a harsh response. Here are some options:

1. If the judgments are accurate and not harsh, you will learn from them and not get triggered.

2. If the judgments are accurate but harsh, you will learn from them, and you will say something like the following: "I appreciate your feedback, but I would prefer if you could convey it in a more kindly way."

3. If the judgments are inaccurate, you will assert yourself in standing up for your point of view while also looking to find common ground with the person.

4. If necessary, you will set limits on evaluations that are so angry or harsh as to cause you emotional harm. For example, you might say, "It isn't OK to yell at me like that, whether or not you are right."

---

6. In order to be successful with your plan, you may first need to develop your Assertiveness Capacity (http://personal-growth-programs. com/people-pleasing-pattern) or your Limit-Setting Capacity (http:// personal-growth-programs.com/limit-setting-capacity).

Work out this plan and write it here:

_____

_____

_____

_____

Then put it into operation and keep a record of your results. Be aware that it may take time for the plan to succeed.

Once you have worked out your plan, you know that you don't need to get extreme about trying to make your work perfect. You can make a reasonable effort and then turn in your project.

The Creative-Block Perfectionist

Wisdom of the Ease Capacity

a. Mistakes are a natural part of the process of learning. In fact, you can learn from your mistakes. When you are learning something, you can't expect to do it well at first. This doesn't mean that there is something wrong with you. You are practicing in order to hone your skills. It will never again be a difficult as it is at first. It will get easier and easier as time goes on.

b. In the process of experimenting or developing something new and innovative, you will naturally make mistakes. Your work won't be high quality at first. In fact, this is not a time to be concerned with quality or excellence. Such concerns would disrupt the creative process. This is a time to be free, open, and creative. Such an attitude will lead to high quality in the future.

c. Mistakes are a natural part of creating anything. It is rare for a piece of work to come out perfect at first. Usually the best approach is to produce a series of rough drafts of increasing quality until your work is good enough for your purposes.

Working Through the Fears of the Creative-Block Perfectionist

This type of Perfectionist Pattern tends to be activated when you are learning a skill or gaining new knowledge, or

when you are experimenting in a creative way with a new endeavor. Your Perfectionist Pattern makes you afraid to come up with or produce anything because it may not be very good at first, and that is frightening.

Sarah, the woman with writer's block from Chapter 1, is an example of this type of Perfectionist.

There are two possibilities in this situation:

1. No one will see what you produce. In this case, you are safe from criticism. Initially you will be producing work that may not be very good, but that is to be expected, and it may even be necessary for your learning or experimenting. These are just rough drafts and will be improved or even

rewritten many times as you go. This means that you don't have to worry about their quality at all. You won't show your work to anyone until you have improved it to the point at which it is very good, and therefore you will be safe.

You may say that you don't care about other people's opinions and that **you** are the one who doesn't want your work to be poor or mediocre. However, this simply means that you haven't uncovered your underlying Perfectionist fears yet. Once you do, it will become apparent that your attitudes originate in a fear of other people's reactions.

Write here how you know that the situation is safe because you won't be showing your work to anyone:

_____

_____

_____

_____

For example, Sarah worked on remembering that that no one was going to see the rough drafts of her writing. She knew she would eventually be evaluated, but she kept reminding herself that that was far in the future. This helped her to relax and not be so concerned about the quality of her initial efforts.

2. You will be showing your work to a teacher, to colleagues, or to someone else. In this case, remember that these people know that your work is at an early stage or that you are just learning or experimenting. They don't expect you to be excellent yet. If they do criticize your work, it is just aimed at helping you learn or improve what you are

doing. Therefore, you can relax and operate without being concerned about your output. What do you know about the life situation that makes it safe to not be perfectionistic?

_____

_____

_____

_____

Even if one of these people is harsh and you do get judged or shamed, you can handle that. You are resilient and self-supporting; you won't fall apart. You have many more internal and external resources for dealing with this situation than you did as a child. Work out a plan for handling this, as explained above under the Not-Enough Perfectionist, and write it here:

_____

_____

_____

_____

Your Perfectionist Pattern **does** have an important role to play in helping you to improve your work, but this input must come at the right time, which is after you have produced something that is far enough along that it is ready for evaluation. Then you can criticize what you have done and help yourself improve it, like a good coach. If you are writing, this shouldn't happen after each sentence but only later, when you have finished a draft of what you are producing.

Then criticism will be helpful. If you are in the early stages of a project, if you are just learning a skill, or if you are experimenting with something new, a critique probably isn't called for yet. It will be needed later on when your work is somewhat polished. Most importantly, by holding off until then, the critique won't get in the way of your learning or creativity.

This is why there are rules for brainstorming. Everyone generates ideas, and no one is allowed to state any criticisms. Only after all the ideas are out can they be evaluated.

Let's go back to Sarah. After she had finished a rough draft of her writing, she allowed herself to critique it and make changes. Then she rewrote the draft, again not allowing her Perfectionist Inner Critic to interfere until she was finished. After that, she evaluated her work again. She went through many rounds like this until her writing attained the high quality she was looking for.

The Control Perfectionist

Wisdom of the Ease Capacity

Uncertainty and nonlinear flow are major parts of life. You will often be in situations in which you don't know the exact right answer or you don't have enough information to be sure about how to proceed. Often the right way can only be found by trial and error or by nonlinear play and creativity.

Working Through the Fears of the Control Perfectionist

You may have grown up in a world of chaos and perceived danger, where everything was unpredictable. So your inner world became chaotic and overwhelming. Un-

consciously you are stuck back there, in some sense. You might feel an extreme need for order and predictability in your current life to prevent this kind of chaos.

However, you current life probably isn't like that. You have become an adult and have created a different life for yourself—one that is more stable. Or if there is some chaos, you have a much greater ability to handle it than you did as a child.

Therefore, you don't have to try to be perfect to ward off chaos. You can relax and allow your life to unfold in an easier way, without the danger of things getting out of control. Write here what about your current life makes it safe to not be perfectionistic:

_____

_____

_____

_____

Try this out and see what happens. You will realize that it is OK to relax and take it easy.

The Ease Capacity

Now let's take a deeper look at the Ease Capacity. You read earlier in this chapter that ease means accomplishing tasks in a relaxed, easy way, without stress or striving. Here are some aspects of the Ease Capacity. Think about which ones you want to develop.

- ❐ Not being overly attached to outcomes
- ❐ Going through life in a relaxed way, without pushing, yet still making progress with my work
- ❐ Being present in each moment
- ❐ Trusting my competence
- ❐ Paying attention to my breath and what I notice in the moment, without being distracted by a sense of urgency or a to-do list
- ❐ Doing my work in a way that flows
- ❐ Feeling pleasure and lightness as I do my work
- ❐ Trusting my ability to learn new skills
- ❐ Taking time for my other needs, such as social time, personal health, fun, and relaxation
- ❐ Trusting myself to experiment with new ideas
- ❐ Completing my work without forcing it to be perfect, instead noticing when it feels "good enough" and allowing it to come to a natural completion

What aspects of the Ease Capacity would you like to develop more? Write them here:

_____

_____

_____

_____

A Story of Developing the Ease Capacity

This continuation of Jeremy's story shows how he developed his Ease Capacity after using the Working-Through approach in this chapter.

When Jeremy started working on these issues in therapy, he learned that his Perfectionist was in fact trying to protect him. It believed that if it forced him to make his work really perfect, he could prove to his boss that he was a success and deserved appreciation and love.

Jeremy realized that he was behaving as if his boss was his father. He knew that although his father had been harsh and critical, his boss was a pretty nice guy who seemed fairly approachable when Jeremy wasn't in the grip of his fear.

JEREMY: "I did a reality check on the reactions I was expecting from my boss. I've seen him in a lot of different situations at work, and he's never flown off the handle like my father used to. I made a checklist of my fears, and I realized that none of them were going to happen with my boss—they were all about my father. I was playing an old tape over and over, and it was time to let it go. I asked my Perfectionist to see that my father was no longer a threat, and it agreed."

Jeremy asked for a private meeting with his boss and explained that he wasn't clear about his boss's standards for his work. He asked if his boss would be willing to give him feedback about a project so he could find out where the bar was. He assured his boss that this information would go a long way toward helping him meet his deadlines. Jeremy's boss agreed to his request and was happy to see Jeremy taking initiative to resolve the problem.

JEREMY: "At first it was hard to talk to my boss, but I knew it was the only way out of my old pattern. I was never going to break the pattern unless I tried something different. It was really exciting to see that I could take initiative and create a different outcome. It helped me feel a lot more self-confidence."

Over time, Jeremy's boss communicated the standard of work he expected, and Jeremy learned that he didn't have to be perfect to do a good job. His fears died down as he discovered that his work was adequate. Also, even when his boss did express criticism, he did it in a respectful, professional manner that didn't threaten Jeremy.

Jeremy began to get excellent reviews from his boss, and his career flourished.

Note: It isn't always as easy to change a Perfectionist Pattern as it was in the examples in this book. Sometimes it requires a longer time and working through more obstacles. If this is your situation, don't become resigned. Make sure to give it enough time and effort for the change to happen.[7]

Higher Accomplishment

In the Pattern System, in addition to healthy capacities, there are higher capacities, which are the more evolved or spiritual aspects of the capacities or dimensions. When you are living from a higher capacity, you embody a version of the capacity that is less egocentric and more oriented toward the good of the whole. You are living from a place that is informed by the sense that we are all connected, and you care for this larger unity.

The Higher Accomplishment Capacity is an integration of the higher aspects of Ease and Work Confidence. It has the following aspects:

Process Is Fulfilling

Your work flows naturally because you aren't attached to its outcome. You are passionate about your work for its own sake. The process is what is important. You are so fully engaged in the process that it is fulfilling in itself, so the work just flows effortlessly.

Which of these aspects would you like to develop more?

❐ Work flowing easily and naturally

❐ Lack of attachment to outcome of projects

❐ Passion about the work for its own sake

---

7. If it still isn't working, you might want to consider taking one of our Perfectionism or IFS classes or going into IFS therapy. See Appendix D for these resources.

❐ Feeling fulfilled by the process independent of the outcome

Life Purpose

You are committed to excellent work, but not because you care about being successful and admired. Your work has a higher purpose—it's your calling in life to contribute to the betterment of other people, the environment, or society. You feel passionate about bringing your gifts to the world and making a difference.

Which of these aspects would you like to develop more?

❐ Having a sense of life purpose

❐ Feeling passionate about bringing my gifts to the world

Flowing with the Universe

You are in touch with the flow of the universe and you participate in it, cocreating it and following it at the same time. You plan for the future, but you recognize that your plans may have to change according to circumstances, feedback, and your arising sense of what is called for, so you are open to changing your strategies at any moment. When plans aren't necessary, you are able to flow with each moment, taking the action that is needed according to the situation and your deeper sense of purpose.

Which of these aspects would you like to develop more?

❐ Ability to change plans according to new information

❐ Ability to flow with each moment

CHAPTER 6

Your Perfectionist Inner Critic
and Ease Inner Champion

If your Perfectionist Pattern includes an Inner Critic side, this means that in addition to being overly perfectionistic, you also have a part of you that judges and shames you when it thinks you aren't perfect enough or your work isn't of high enough quality.

You don't have to live under the attacks of that voice any more. You can develop an aspect of yourself that we call the Inner Champion, which supports and encourages you. It is a magic bullet for dealing with the negative impact of any Inner Critic,[8] including the Perfectionist version. The Inner Champion doesn't try to argue with the Critic or banish it. Your Inner Champion supports you in being yourself and feeling good about yourself in the face of Critic messages.

In the face of a Perfectionist Critic, your Ease Inner

---

8. See our book *Activating Your Inner Champion Instead of Your Inner Critic.*

Champion supports you in developing the Ease Capacity. It affirms your right to not be perfect. It reminds you that it is only human to make mistakes, and making an error doesn't mean that anything is wrong with you. It reminds you that you are totally OK even if you don't get everything right.

Your Inner Champion supports your right to have balance in your life—to rest, take care of yourself, and enjoy life. It has the wisdom to know that sometimes it is important to go with the flow and let things evolve rather than trying to get everything perfect right away. It supports you in being a learner who doesn't have to know everything right from the start. It knows the meaning of "rough draft."

Meeting Your Inner Champion

Visit http://www.personalgrowthapplication.com/Pattern/PerfectionistPatternWorkbook/Perfectionist_Pattern_Workbook_Meditation.aspx to engage in a guided meditation in which you meet your Perfectionist (Ease) Inner Champion. This will prepare you for profiling it.

Visit http://psychemaps.com/Profile to go to a program on our website that goes with this ebook that will allow you to profile your Perfectionist Inner Critic. (This is a different program from the web workbook.) You will also be able to choose an image or two that represent what your Inner Critic looks like (or upload your own). This program will also allow you to profile your Ease Inner Champion (which, in this program, is called the Perfectionist Inner Champion).

Statements from Your Inner Champion

The following are common statements that people want to hear from their Perfectionist Inner Champion. They are arranged by these four aspects of the Inner Champion:

1. **Boundary Setting.** Your Inner Champion helps you to set limits on your Inner Critic.

2. **Nurturing.** Your Inner Champion nurtures the parts of you that have been hurt by your Critic.

3. **Guidance.** Your Inner Champion provides guidance and perspective in seeing yourself and your choices clearly despite the Critic's distortions.

4. **Action Planning.** Your Inner Champion helps you make plans to move ahead successfully despite your Critic's doubts and blocks.

Check off the statements below that you'd like to hear from your Perfectionist Inner Champion.

Boundary-Setting Statements

❐ Enough is enough!

❐ It's not the end of the world.

❐ Please back off and give me some space to think, find my center, and set my priorities.

❐ If you want to have input, please find a way to state it more positively.

Nurturing Statements

❐ Take care of yourself.

❐ Remember to keep yourself in balance.

❐ You are what is really important.

☐ Everything doesn't have to be perfect—some things can be good enough.

☐ You can cut yourself some slack.

☐ You are not defined by how perfect things seem.

☐ Just get started. You can course-correct along the way.

☐ Life is a rough draft.

Guidance Statements

☐ You can trust in yourself and your capacities.

☐ You can ask for help or guidance.

☐ I'll help you keep a list of human resources handy so you can access help when needed.

☐ Hold a larger perspective about where you are on your life journey. Don't sweat the small stuff.

☐ You are who you are. The perfection of those you love is not a reflection on you.

☐ Others aren't perfect, and you can't make them be.

☐ You can only really control yourself.

☐ It's important to balance focus and relaxation.

☐ Creativity never emerges flawlessly.

Action Planning Statements

☐ Ready-Fire-Aim can be the best motto. It's OK to course-correct and learn from your mistakes.

☐ Keep your larger vision in sight as you move through what has to be done.

☐ Check with others early and often so you feel confident about your work as you go.

❒ Keep ALL of you in mind as you make your decisions.

❒ Know when to hold on and when to let go.

Visit http://psychemaps.com/Profile to go to the Profile Program for your Perfectionist Inner Critic, as mentioned earlier. Now you can check off the various statements listed above (and add your own) in order to profile your Perfectionist Inner Champion. These might be statements that you already hear inside or ones that you are beginning to hear more often. Or they can simply be statements that you would like to hear from your Inner Champion, even if this hasn't happened up to this point.

You will also be able to choose among various images of what you would like your Inner Champion to look like, or upload your own. This will allow you to create a complete profile of your Perfectionist (Ease) Inner Champion. You will be able to print out and use this profile to practice activating your Inner Champion to help support you at those times in your life when your Perfectionist Inner Critic is attacking you, along with activating your Ease Capacity. See the next chapter for this practice.

Chapter 7

Practicing Behavior Change

This chapter presents "real-time" practice where you can work on evoking your Ease Capacity to replace your Perfectionist Pattern.

This is where the rubber meets the road! This is the practice that can change your relationship, and we have provided lots of support for you to make this happen, including the web workbook[9] and the Perfectionism Online Community.[10]

Practice Outline

Here is a brief outline of the steps in this chapter:

1. Know why you want to do this practice.

2. Choose a life situation to practice on.

3. Know when your Perfectionism gets triggered.

4. Remind yourself that Perfectionism isn't necessary.

5. Create Ease.

6. Get support for your practice.

7. Track and improve your practice.

---

9. http://www.personalgrowthapplication.com/Pattern/Perfectionist PatternWorkbook/Perfectionist_Pattern_Workbook.aspx
10. http://www.personal-growth-programs.com/connect

Clarifying Your Intention for Doing the Practice

Before you engage in this practice, it is helpful to clearly have in mind what you intend to gain by making this change. It is not enough to just decide that it would be a good thing to do. Figure out why you want to do it, set an intention for your practice, and keep this in mind during the week. This will help you discipline yourself to stick to the practice.

Think through the pain and difficulties caused by your Perfectionist Pattern.

Notice those that will motivate you to change:

- ❐ I feel broken.
- ❐ I feel inadequate.
- ❐ I feel worthless.
- ❐ I feel wrong.
- ❐ I feel stupid.
- ❐ I feel ashamed.
- ❐ I feel judged.

❒ I feel angry.

❒ I feel lazy.

❒ I feel criticized.

❒ I feel bad (not good enough).

❒ I don't feel valued.

❒ I feel overworked.

❒ I feel pressured.

❒ I feel like I must be perfect.

❒ I feel pushed.

❒ Other pain and difficulties _____

_____

_____

What do you have to gain from living from Ease Capacity in your life, especially those things you really want?

❒ Feeling good enough

❒ Feeling better about myself

❒ Feeling relief

❒ Feeling relaxed

❒ Feeling valued

❒ Feeling accepted

❒ Feeling respected

❒ Feeling strong and capable

❒ Feeling light and at ease while I do my work

❒ Feeling more enjoyment of my life

❒ Feeling more present

❐ Feeling appreciation for what IS

❐ The ability to celebrate small victories as well as big ones

❐ The ability to think positively more often

❐ The ability to complete my work without being stressed

❐ The ability to get things done on time

❐ The freedom of letting go of outcomes

❐ The ability to have better relationships with less judgment

❐ The satisfying experience of reaching resolutions

❐ Other things to gain _____

_____

_____

Planning Ahead

Think of a situation that is coming up in the next week or so, or one that arises frequently, in which you want to practice the Ease Capacity. Or instead, think of a situation in which you typically become perfectionistic and would like to change that. For example:

- I can't stop thinking about what I have to do.
- I start obsessing about a project.
- I become irritable.
- I forget to eat.
- I can't get started on a project

Let's call this the *life situation.* If you aren't sure when your Perfectionist Pattern gets triggered or if it seems to be around a lot of the time, then leave the life situation blank and work on noticing **whenever** that pattern is activated.

As you read through the rest of this chapter, fill in your answers in the Workbook. The Workbook will produce a report page that tells you what you plan to do during your life to engage in this practice. You can carry this page of the Workbook with you by printing it out or keeping it on a mobile device.

You can do this practice more than once if you want to work on more than one life situation. You will have a different Workbook report page for each practice. If this life situation isn't going to come up in the next few weeks, you can do this practice by **imagining** it coming up and how you will change your behavior.

What are you afraid of in this life situation? For example, if you have to give a presentation at work, you might become extremely anxious in anticipation of your boss and co-workers finding fault or discovering that you haven't done enough preparation.

You may have a few specific aspects of Ease that you want to develop in this life situation. For example, you might want to develop the ability to calmly and realistically assess whether your preparation for a presentation is adequate. What aspects of Ease do you want to develop in this life situation?

Set an intention to pay close attention during the life situation to see if your Perfectionist Pattern is activated. Or try to notice **whenever** it is activated.

What are the feelings, thoughts, or behaviors that will

cue you that your Perfectionist Pattern is activated? For example, "I want to stay home from work," "My mind goes blank," "I get dry mouth," or "My stomach is in knots."

Remember the target fear for this life situation. To the extent that it isn't true, what is true instead? What are some statements that will remind you that your target fear won't really happen or that your negative perception isn't accurate? Choose from among the following statements, or create your own:

- ❐ I've done a lot of work in preparation for this presentation.
- ❐ My boss has confidence in my work.
- ❐ I'm good at what I do. I know my stuff.
- ❐ My coworkers respect me and sometimes even seek me out for guidance.
- ❐ If someone criticizes an aspect of my presentation, I know how to support my ideas and respond professionally.
- ❐ I work with a bunch of great people who want me to succeed.
- ❐ If I make mistakes, I can learn from them.
- ❐ Other statements _____

_____

_____

If there is some validity to your fears or perceptions, remember the plan you devised in Chapter 5 to handle that situation. You will put that plan into action this week.

Creating Ease

Which of these statements will encourage you to create the aspects of Ease you want in this life situation?

- ❒ I can let go of trying to force a perfect outcome.
- ❒ It is possible for me to work in a relaxed way and still make good progress with my work.
- ❒ I really can be present in this moment.
- ❒ I can pay attention to my breath and what I notice in the moment without being distracted by a sense of urgency or a to-do list.
- ❒ I can do my work in a way that flows.
- ❒ I can feel pleasure and lightness as I do my work.

❐ I can take time for my other needs, such as social time and personal health needs, and balance these with my work.

❐ I can notice when my work feels "good enough" and allow it to come to a natural completion from there.

❐ It's OK to be learning something new and not be good at it yet.

❐ Other statements _____

_____

_____

Which of the following statements would you like your Ease Inner Champion to say to you?

❐ You are OK even if you're not perfect.

❐ You deserve to have time for fun, relaxation, friends, and family.

❐ It's OK to do this, even though you may make mistakes at first.

❐ You are competent.

❐ You don't have to be the best at everything.

❐ You do excellent work.

❐ You deserve to have an easy time with your work.

❐ Your work will be very good when it is finished.

❐ It's OK to be a beginner and not know everything.

❐ You will be very good once you have learned this new skill.

❐ Flow and creativity are just as important as excellence.

❑ It's exciting to experiment with new things, and perfection isn't important.

❑ It's sometimes OK to be "good enough."

❑ Love, family, and community are more important than looking good.

❑ Other statements _____

_____

_____

What body sensation, feeling, or state of consciousness will help you evoke these aspects of Ease (for example, that sense of satisfaction when you know you've done enough on a project and can move on to other things; the excitement of starting a new project without fear; or an easy, relaxed feeling of confidence in your ability)? _____

_____

_____

_____

What image will help create Ease (for example, lying on your back in a grassy field with arms outstretched or gliding on water skis)? _____

_____

_____

_____

Can any people close to you help you create Ease? What help do you want from them (for example, to respond supportively and with lightness when you make a mistake)?

_____

_____

_____

Is there something you want people close to you to stop doing (for example, teasing you when your Perfectionist gets triggered)? _____

_____

_____

Talk to the people close to you about what they can do (or stop doing) that will help you activate the Ease Capacity and especially the aspects of Ease you want in this life situation.

Your Ease Practice Workbook Section

There is a separate section of the web workbook for helping you engage in your Ease Practice and keep track of it. The rest of this chapter explains how to engage in this practice and use this section.

Working with a Buddy

People have much more success with practices like this if they have a "buddy" to witness them and be their cheerleader. We recommend that you find a friend who is a good listener and who will understand what you are doing and be supportive. Or join our Perfectionism Online Community,[11] where we will help you find a buddy.

After you make your plans for the practice, call your buddy and talk through what you will be doing. If you have written down specific words you want to say in the situation, practice saying them to your buddy. Even role-play the situation. Have your buddy play your boss or a coworker while you practice interacting with him or her in a way that would create the ease you want.

Set a time frame for checking in with your buddy on your progress with the practice. You could just do it once at the end of a week to report on how the practice has gone. But for even more effective support, consider checking in with your buddy every two or three days, or even every day, to let him or her know how it is going. The act of reporting in will really help keep you on track. When you know that you'll be talking to someone about your practice, you're much more likely to do it and to keep track of what happened.

When the Life Situation Occurs

With some life situations, you know ahead of time when they will happen. For example, you know when you will be preparing to go out to an important social function. In these cases, take some time right before this happens to go to Ease Practice Plans[12] in the web workbook (or review the pages in the paperback workbook) and the Profile Program[13] to review how you want to handle this life situation. (Keep in

---

11. http://www.personal-growth-programs.com/connect
12. http://www.personalgrowthapplication.com/Pattern/Perfectionist PatternWorkbook/Perfectionist_Pattern_Workbook_Practice_Plans. aspx?pname=LifeSituation
13. http://psychemaps.com/Profile

mind that the web workbook and the Profile Program are two different programs.) If you don't have time right before it happens, take some time earlier to prepare.

Some situations allow you to process this material **during** the life situation. For example, if the life situation involves working right up to the last minute on a project, you can take a time-out from the work, process the Perfectionist feelings that are coming up, and then return to your work and put your plan into operation. In this case, when you take the time-out, click the above two links to review how you plan to handle the situation so you can decide what to do.

During the life situation, pay close attention and notice the feelings, thoughts, or behaviors that will cue you that your Perfectionist Pattern is activated.

If it is triggered, do the following:

- Say the statements (out loud or silently) that will remind you that you don't have to be afraid of Ease, or create your own on the spot.

- Put your plan into action to assert yourself around the possibility of harm or rejection.

- Say the statements (out loud or silently) that will inspire you to create Ease, or create your own on the spot.

- Use a body sensation, feeling, or state of consciousness (if you have chosen one) to help create Ease.

- Look at the image you have chosen (if you have one) to inspire you to create Ease.

- Say the statements you would like to hear from your Perfectionist Inner Champion.

- Look at the image(s) for your Perfectionist Inner Champion.

If you were successful in creating Ease, celebrate your success! Give yourself a pat on the back or a reward, such a relaxing warm bath. Appreciate yourself for this step in changing your behavior. It is very important to reinforce each step, however small, in the right direction.

After the situation has happened, enter your Practice Notes (see below) as soon as you have time to enter what happened. Or if you don't have time, do it at the end of the day when doing your Daily Check-In Notes.

If you came up with new statements, add them to your workbook to use in the future. If you have additional insights into any of the material you have filled out previously in the workbook, feel free to add them to the pages you have already filled out.

Practice Notes

Enter your answers according to what you did in your practice. (Not all need to be answered.)

The life situation _____

_____

_____

The fears that came up in this situation _____

_____

_____

The aspects of Ease you were working on developing in this

situation _____

_____

_____

What triggered the Perfectionist Pattern _____

_____

_____

The statements you said to remind yourself that you don't

have to be afraid of Ease _____

_____

_____

_____

What you did to assert yourself to handle harm or rejection

_____

_____

_____

The statements you said to yourself to inspire you to create

Ease _____

_____

_____

The body sensation, feeling, or state of consciousness you used to help create Ease _____

_____

_____

The image you used to inspire you to create Ease _____

_____

_____

The statements your Perfectionist Inner Champion said to you _____

_____

_____

The image(s) of your Perfectionist Inner Champion _____

_____

_____

How you did in attempting to create Ease _____

_____

_____

Further notes on what happened _____

_____

_____

_____

Is there anything you want to do differently next time?

_____

_____

_____

Daily Check-In

In order to remember to do this practice, it will help you to check in with yourself once a day in addition to any checking in you do with your buddy. Choose a time when you will have a few minutes to yourself and when it will be easy for you to remember to check in each day. For many people, this is right before going to bed each night or upon waking each morning. But in all cases, choose a consistent time of day that works best for you.

If the life situation only occurs once a week or a few times a month, you don't need to enter Daily Check-In Notes every day. Just reflect to see if it happened that day and take notes if it did. On the days it didn't happen, you don't need to do anything.

Take notes on what you were aware of that day. If the life situation occurred, write down what happened. Enter these below.

Reflect on whether the Perfectionist Pattern was activated today, whether you noticed and did the practice, and what happened. _____

_____

_____

Did the life situation happen today? _____

_____

_____

If so, were you paying attention when it happened? _____

_____

Did the Perfectionist Pattern get triggered today (in that situation or any other one)? _____

If so, did you notice when the Perfectionist Pattern was triggered today? _____

If you didn't, what kept you from noticing? _____

_____

_____

_____

What can you do tomorrow to help you be more aware?

_____

_____

_____

If you did notice that the Perfectionist Pattern was triggered,

did you do the practice to evoke Ease? _____

If not, what stopped you from doing that? _____

_____

_____

What can you do next time to help yourself remember to

evoke Ease? _____

_____

_____

If you did the practice and didn't track what happened at the time, enter it under Practice Notes. If you did it more than once, take separate notes for each instance by clicking that link multiple times.

Is there anything you want to do differently tomorrow or the next time the Perfectionist Pattern is triggered?

_____

_____

_____

Weekly Check-In

After a week, take notes on how this practice is working.

Day of week _____

How many times did you do the practice this week? _____

Was this enough to be helpful to you? _____

If you did the practice enough, how much of a difference
did it make? _____

_____

What worked in doing the practice? _____

_____

_____

_____

What didn't work in doing the practice? _____

_____

_____

_____

Do you want to do the practice again next week? _____

Is there anything you want to do differently next week?

_____

_____

_____

Chapter 8

The Accomplishment Dimension

The information in this chapter will help you to get a fuller sense of the various patterns and healthy capacities you might have with respect to accomplishment. You might learn about other patterns you want to explore and may see the relationships between your patterns and capacities. However, if you aren't interested in this level of complexity, feel free to skip this chapter or come back to it at a later time.

The Accomplishment Dimension

The Perfectionist Pattern is part of the *Accomplishment Dimension* in the Pattern System. Let's look at how it is related to the other patterns and capacities.

There are five problematic interpersonal patterns in the Accomplishment Dimension—Taskmaster, Procrastination, Resigned, Perfectionist, and Sloppy.[14]

- The **Taskmaster Pattern** involves pushing yourself unmercifully to overwork, often in an attempt to be very successful, and judging yourself harshly whenever you don't.

- The **Procrastination Pattern** involves avoiding tasks that need to be done.

---

14. There will be books on most of these patterns. Visit http://personal-growth-programs.com/pattern-system/pattern-system-series to see if they are available.

- The **Resigned Pattern** involves not having confidence that you can accomplish your goals or get anywhere in life and therefore not trying to do anything or be anything.

- The **Perfectionist Pattern** involves believing you must always do everything perfectly and that it's never okay to make a mistake.

- The **Sloppy Pattern** involves caring very little about your work and appearance, doing as little as possible, and having low standards.

Two healthy capacities—Ease and Work Confidence—are related to these four patterns.

- **Ease**, as discussed previously, is the ability to accomplish tasks in a relaxed, easy way without stress or striving.

- **Work Confidence** is about being confident and able to work well, accomplish tasks, and produce excellent work, with deep caring and devotion for what you produce, and taking pride in the great work you create.

Work Confidence is a complement to Ease. For healthy accomplishment, you need both capacities. Ease helps you to relax and your work to flow, and with Work Confidence, you feel strong about your gifts and ability to be productive on the job. If you have Work Confidence, you easily engage in tasks that need to be done. You are clear and careful in your work and can work hard to achieve your goals, but without overstriving.

This is the nature of healthy capacities—they naturally integrate with each other, which means that they don't oppose each other. They work together; they both support your flourishing in achievement-related areas of your life. If you have both capacities, you are able to relax while at the same time being confident that you can successfully apply yourself when called for.

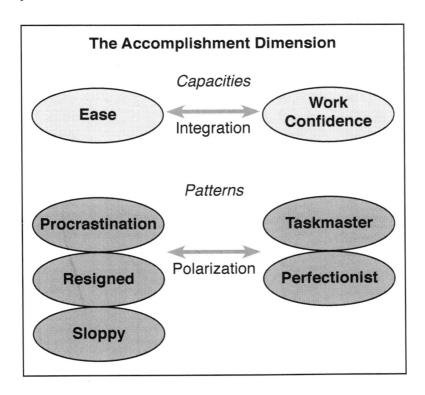

Relations Between the Patterns and Capacities

Patterns in Conflict

The patterns on the left and right sides don't integrate with each other in the way the healthy capacities do. They are polarized, which means they battle each other to determine how you get tasks done. On the one hand, the Procrastination Pattern involves avoiding doing work, and the Resigned Pattern involves having no initiative. While on the other hand, the Taskmaster Pattern involves driving yourself unnecessarily hard with intense striving and beating yourself up for not working hard enough.

The Sloppy Pattern involves doing poor work and having little to no investment in doing things well, while the Perfectionist Pattern involves an unhealthy obsession with doing things perfectly and judging yourself as never good enough. Another way to look at it is that the three patterns on the left are about *under*functioning, while the two on the right are about *over*functioning.

You might be driven with certain tasks and avoid others. Perhaps you avoid taking on a project for fear of becoming too driven or perfectionistic if you did.

In some cases, paradoxically, a Perfectionist (or Taskmaster) Pattern can actually lead to a lack of Work Confidence. You might have such high standards for achievement or perfection that you feel inadequate because you can never meet them.

Patterns Are Dysfunctional Versions of Capacities

Ease is a healthy version of the Procrastination, Resigned, and Sloppy Patterns. Another way to say this is that those three are extreme, dysfunctional versions of Ease. They are attempts to feel okay by staying away from work that could be criticized, or to attain relaxation and fun by avoiding work or being apathetic about achievement.

The same applies on the right side. Work Confidence is a healthy version of the Taskmaster and the Perfectionist. Or you can say that the Taskmaster and Perfectionist Patterns are extreme, dysfunctional versions of Work Confidence. The Taskmaster and Perfectionist try to make you work hard and be successful and perfect by pushing and judging you.

Capacities Resolve Patterns

If you have the Procrastination, Resigned, or Sloppy Pattern, Work Confidence is what you need to develop to break away from them. Thus the capacity on the opposite side of the graphic is the one needed to transform a pattern. In order to get there, you will need the courage to face and work through your fears, develop confidence in your talents and abilities, practice follow-through, and apply yourself to achieve goals.

The same applies on the other side. If you have a Taskmaster or Perfectionist Pattern, you need Ease to break free from it. That's why Ease is emphasized in this book on Perfectionism. When you develop a sense of ease, you'll trust that you can accomplish your goals without driving yourself all the time.

Here is another graphic showing these relationships:

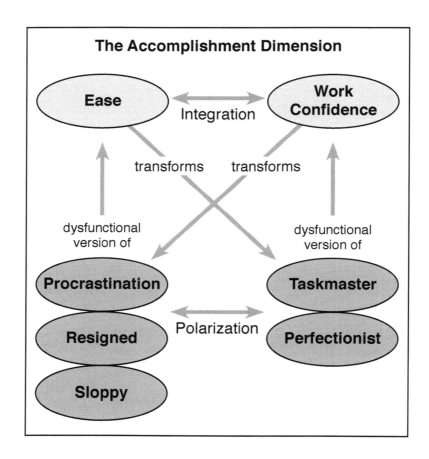

The Accomplishment Dimension

Ease ←→ Work Confidence

Integration

transforms   transforms

dysfunctional version of   dysfunctional version of

Procrastination   Taskmaster

Resigned   Polarization   Perfectionist

Sloppy

Questionnaire

It would be helpful to track which of the patterns and capacities in this dimension you have. You may have an idea from reading the descriptions, or you can take a quiz on our website. This questionnaire will give you a score for each of the patterns and capacities in the Accomplishment Dimension to help clarify how strongly you have the Perfectionist Pattern or each of the other patterns in that dimension. It will also tell you how high you score on the healthy capacities in that dimension. To take this quiz, visit http://www.personalgrowthapplication.com/Members/Questionnaire.aspx?Questionnaire=10.

CHAPTER 9

Conclusion

Deep Healing and Transformation
of the Perfectionist Pattern

When we do psychotherapy with our clients, we use
Internal Family Systems Therapy (IFS), a very powerful, cutting-edge approach developed by pioneering psychologist Richard Schwartz, PhD. Since we discovered IFS
a decade ago, we have seen amazing results in our clients'
lives. Jay was developing the Pattern System for more than
a decade before he discovered IFS and was thrilled to find
that the two are a natural fit.

IFS work can complement the work you do on your Perfectionist Pattern using this book. IFS would help you to
experientially access the motivations and childhood origins
behind this pattern and to heal and transform the pattern.
Then your homework practice on developing your Ease Capacity would be even more effective. If you want to experience the most profound and lasting change in your pattern,
we recommend that you practice IFS with your Perfectionist Part as described below.

The IFS Model

IFS enables you to understand each of the *parts* of your
psyche, sometimes called *subpersonalities*. Think of them as
little people inside you. Each has its own perspective, feel-

ings, memories, goals, and motivations. And sometimes they are at odds with each other. For example, one part of you might be trying to lose weight, and another part might want to eat whatever you want. We all have many different parts, such as the procrastinator, the lover, the inner critic, the lonely child, the rebel, the caretaker, and so on.

If you have the Perfectionist Pattern, there is a part of you that believes you should never make a mistake. You can use IFS to work on your Perfectionist Part as well as any other patterns you have.

IFS recognizes that we all have child parts that are in pain, which are called *exiles.* These correspond to the wounds in the Pattern System. The parts that try to keep us from feeling this pain are called *protectors,* which correspond to the patterns.

Most important, IFS recognizes that we all have a true *Self,* which is our core healthy place or spiritual center. IFS has some innovative and easy ways to access Self. You get to know your parts and develop trusting relationships with them from the place of Self, which then leads to healing and transformation of those parts.

The IFS Process with Your Perfectionist Part

IFS is an experiential therapy. You don't just get insight into your parts. You actually go inside, contact them, and have conversations with them.

What follows is a brief description of how you would do IFS with your Perfectionist Part. It is just an overview to give you an idea of how the process works. The actual procedure is much more detailed and specialized. We don't expect you to be able to do IFS by reading this brief description. You will need to learn how to engage in the IFS process using my book *Self-Therapy* or classes, or by going into individual therapy with an IFS therapist (see Appendix D).

First you access your Perfectionist Part experientially. You might feel it emotionally, or hear its words, or get a mental image of what it looks like. Then you access Self so that you are separate from your Perfectionist Part and have a place to stand from which to connect with it. You make sure that you are open to getting to know it from its own perspective rather than judging it or wanting to get rid of it.

Then you ask it to tell you what it is trying to accomplish for you by keeping you focused on trying to be perfect. You want to know what it is afraid would happen if it allowed you to not be perfect. This helps you to recognize the exile (wounded inner child part) that it is protecting.

This conversation will give you a good sense of how the Perfectionist Part is trying to protect you, even if that protection isn't really needed anymore. This allows you to appreciate its efforts on your behalf, and your appreciation helps the Perfectionist Part to trust you.

You ask the Perfectionist Part for permission to work with the exile it is protecting. Then you get to know that child part and find out what happened when you were young to cause that part to be so afraid and wounded. You witness these memories in an experiential way (you may or may not know them already)—that is, you see them in a mental movie of your past. Then you enter the childhood scene and give that little child what he or she needed back then. Or you protect the wounded child part from being harmed. You might also take that part out of that harmful or painful childhood situation and into your present life, where he or she will be safe and can be connected to you and receive your love and caring.

You help the exile to release the pain and fear that he or she has been carrying all these years. Once this is done, your Perfectionist Part won't feel the need to protect the exile anymore, so it can now relax and stop trying to make you perfect. Then you will be able to have the perspective, balance, and ease you want in your life.

My book *Self-Therapy* describes in detail how to use IFS to work through any psychological issue. See www.selfleadership.org for detailed information about IFS and professional training in the Model. We (and colleagues) also offer classes in which you can learn how to use IFS to work on yourself and do peer counseling with other people from the class. See Appendix D for IFS resources.

Conclusion

We hope this book will help you to transform your Perfectionist Pattern so you can have the ease, fun, and productivity you desire. In order for this to happen, it is important that you fully engage in the practice of creating Ease in Chapter 7. Reading this material and understanding yourself is an important step, but most people need to consciously work on putting this into practice in their lives.

You also may need to work on other patterns of yours in order to fully let go of Perfectionism. Your Perfectionist Pattern may be linked to a Controlling Pattern, a Judgmental Pattern, or one of the others that are mentioned in this book. You may be able to create the Ease you want by only focusing on your Perfectionist Pattern, but you might need to do more to achieve success. If this is the case, read other books in this series, or use the web application when it becomes available, or find other ways to work on those patterns.

Don't become discouraged if your pattern doesn't transform right away. Personal growth isn't a simple, easy process, despite what some self-help books would have you believe. Letting go of a deep-seated problem takes time, effort, and a commitment to work on yourself.

Personal growth is an exciting journey, with twists and turns, painful revelations, unexpected insights, profound shifts, and an ever-deepening sense of self-awareness and mastery. We hope that this book contributes to your personal evolution and the deep satisfaction that comes from living a life of ease and productivity.

The Pattern System^{SM}

The Perfectionist Pattern and the Accomplishment Dimension that contains it are just one small part of the overall Pattern System. You can use the Pattern System to obtain a complete map of your psyche. You will be able to see your strengths and your defenses, your places of pain and how you compensate for them. You'll come to understand the structure of your inner conflicts and see where you are ready to grow. The Pattern System makes clear what you need to explore next in order to resolve the issues that are most important to you.

The goal of working with the Pattern System is to live from your *True Self,* which is who you naturally are when you aren't operating from patterns and when you have developed skills for healthy relating and functioning. Ease is one aspect of the True Self.

A more advanced goal is to live from your *Higher Self,* which is your spiritual ground and the integration of the higher capacities, including Higher Accomplishment.

The Pattern System contains both personal and interpersonal dimensions.

Personal Dimensions in the Pattern System

The Accomplishment Dimension is just one of eleven personal dimensions in the Pattern System, each containing at least two patterns and two capacities. The following are brief descriptions of some of them:

Self-Esteem. Do you feel good about yourself, or do you constantly judge yourself? Do you accept yourself as you are? Do you try to prop up your self-esteem with pride? How do you deal with improving yourself?

Accomplishment. Are you confident in working on and accomplishing tasks? Do you procrastinate? Do you push or judge yourself to try to get things done or to achieve, or can you accomplish with ease?

Pleasure. How do you deal with food, drink, sex, and other bodily pleasures? Do you indulge in harmful ways? Do you control yourself rigidly to avoid doing that? Do you bounce back and forth between overindulging and castigating yourself?

Some further personal dimensions are:

- Action
- Change
- Hope
- Excellence
- Decision
- Risk
- Rationality/Emotion

Each of these dimensions has the same structure as the Accomplishment Dimension. There will be a book on each of the patterns in each dimension. Visit http://personal-growth-programs.com/pattern-system/pattern-system-series to see if they are available.

Interpersonal Dimensions in the Pattern System

The Pattern System also deals with a variety of interpersonal patterns. The following are brief descriptions of some of them:

Conflict. How do you deal with differences of opinion as well as desires, disagreements, judgment, anger, and fights? Do you use avoidance tactics? Do you become angry, blaming, or defensive? Can you communicate your concerns without judgment and own your part in a problem? Do you become frightened or feel bad about yourself? Can you bring up conflicts and set limits on attacks?

Social. How do you relate to people socially? Are you outgoing or shy, scared or confident in reaching out to people or making conversation? Are you self-effacing or charming, attention seeking or avoiding? Are you overly oriented toward performance in the way you relate to others, or are you more genuine?

Care. How do you balance your needs versus other people's needs? Do you end up taking care of others rather than yourself? Do people tell you that you don't show enough care or concern for them?

Intimacy. Do you avoid intimacy, need it too much, fear it, love it? Can you be autonomous in an intimate relationship without denying your needs? Do you get overly dependent in relationships, or can you support yourself?

Power. How do you deal with power in your relationships? Do you give in too easily to others or try too hard to please them? Do you need to be in control? Do you feel as though you must stand up for yourself against people you view as dominating? Do you frustrate others without realizing why? Can you assert yourself? Can you work with people in a spirit of cooperation?

Anger and Strength. How do you deal with self-protection and assertiveness in situations that can bring up anger? Do you dump your anger on people? Do you disown your anger and therefore lose your strength? Can you be centered and communicate clearly when you are angry? Can you be strong and forceful without being reactive?

Trust. Are you usually trusting of people, or do you easily get suspicious? Can you perceive when someone isn't trustworthy, or are you gullible?

Some additional interpersonal dimensions are:

- Honesty
- Evaluation
- Responsibility

Each of these dimensions has the same structure as the Accomplishment Dimension. There will be a book on each of the patterns in each dimension. Visit http://personal-growth-programs.com/pattern-system/pattern-system-series to see which ones are available now.

Wounds

The following are the main wounds:

Harm Wounds

1. Deficiency Wound
2. Betrayal Wound
3. Violation Wound
4. Shame Wound

5. Attack Wound

6. Powerless Wound

7. Exploitation Wound

Rejection Wounds

1. Need Wound

2. Unlovable Wound

3. Deficiency Wound

Other Wounds

1. Dead Wound

2. Fear-of-Disaster Wound

3. Chaos Wound

4. Hopeless Wound

5. Self-Doubt Wound

Motivations

The following are some of the important motivations:

- Fear of Harm
- Fear of Rejection
- Fear of Losing Yourself
- Attempt to Stop Harm
- Attempt to Stop Pain
- Attempt to Get Connection
- Fear of Success
- Fear of Failure
- Opposition to a Parent

An Open-Ended System

The Pattern System is open-ended. We sometimes add new patterns, subpatterns, capacities, and dimensions, or even new types of patterns. We welcome input from other people in developing the Pattern System further. See http://thepatternsystem.wikispaces.com for a fuller outline of the system.

The Seven Types of Inner Critics

We have identified seven types of Inner Critics and learned how to work most effectively with each one. This book deals with the Perfectionist. The other six are as follows:

Inner Controller. The Inner Controller tries to control impulsive behavior that might not be good for you or others.

Taskmaster. The Taskmaster tries to get you to work hard or be disciplined in order to be successful or to avoid being mediocre.

Underminer. The Underminer tries to undermine your self-confidence and self-esteem so you won't take risks where you might fail. It can also try to prevent you from getting too big, powerful, or visible to avoid the threat of attack and rejection.

Destroyer. The Destroyer makes pervasive attacks on your fundamental self-worth. It is deeply shaming and believes you shouldn't exist.

Guilt Tripper. The Guilt-Tripper attacks you for some specific action you have taken (or not taken) in the past. It sometimes makes you feel guilty for repeated behaviors that have been harmful to others or that violate a deeply held value.

Molder. The Molder tries to get you to fit a certain societal mold or act in a certain way that is based on your own family experience or culture. This can be any kind of mold, for example, caring, aggressive, or polite. It attacks you when you don't fit and praises you when you do.

There will be a book on each of these Inner Critics. Visit http://www.personal-growth-programs.com/inner-critic-section/inner-critic-series to see which ones are available.

Definitions of Terms

Dimension. An area of psychological functioning (e.g., power, intimacy, or self-esteem) that contains certain patterns and capacities that deal with similar issues.

Healthy Capacity. A way of behaving or feeling that makes your life productive, connected, and happy. An aspect of the True Self.

Higher Self. Your spiritual ground and the integration of your higher capacities.

Inner Champion. An aspect of yourself that supports and encourages you and helps you feel good about yourself. It is the magic bullet for dealing with the negative impact of the Inner Critic.

Inner Critic. A part of you that judges you, demeans you, and pushes you to do things. It tends to make you feel bad about yourself.

Interpersonal Pattern. A pattern that involves interpersonal relating.

Life Situation. A situation that is coming up in the next week or two in which you will have the opportunity to practice creating a healthy capacity instead of prolonging a pattern.

Motivation. A kind of underlying intention (e.g., fear of harm or desire for approval) that drives a pattern.

Pattern. A way of behaving or feeling that is a problem for you or others (e.g., being dependent, controlling, or judgmental). A pattern tends to be too rigid, extreme, dysfunctional, or inappropriate for the situation you are in.

Polarization. A dynamic in which two patterns are fighting each other to determine how you behave or relate to others.

True Self. Who you naturally are when you aren't operating from patterns and when you have developed skills for healthy relating and functioning. The healthy capacities are aspects of the True Self.

Wound. A harmful or traumatic way you were treated, usually in childhood (e.g., being neglected, hit, or dismissed).

APPENDIX D

Resources

Books

Self-Therapy, by Jay Earley. How to do Internal Family Systems (IFS) sessions on your own or with a partner. Also a manual of the IFS method that can be used by therapists.

Self-Therapy for Your Inner Critic, by Jay Earley and Bonnie Weiss. Applies IFS to working with Inner Critic parts.

Resolving Inner Conflict, by Jay Earley. How to work with polarization using IFS.

Working with Anger in IFS, by Jay Earley. How to work with too much anger or disowned anger using IFS.

Activating Your Inner Champion Instead of Your Inner Critic, by Jay Earley and Bonnie Weiss. How to bring forth your Inner Champion to deal with attacks from your Inner Critic.

Embracing Intimacy, by Jay Earley. How to work through blocks that keep you from having the intimacy you want in your love relationship.

A series of Pattern System books similar to this one will be published over the next few years. A list of the currently available Pattern System books will be maintained and updated at http://www.personal-growth-programs.com/pattern-system-series.

Updates for this book. Visit http://www.personal-growth-programs.com/letting-go-of-perfectionism-owners to register yourself as an owner of this book. You will received an updated version of the book whenever it is improved. You will also be notified about each new book in the series as it comes out.

Classes

We (and our colleagues) teach telephone classes on Perfectionism, Procrastination, and many of the other topics of the Pattern System books. We also teach telephone classes on IFS for the general public. Our website http://www.personal-growth-programs.com has the details.

Websites and Applications

Our IFS website, http://www.personal-growth-programs.com, contains popular and professional articles on IFS and its application to various psychological issues. You can also sign up for our email list to receive future articles and notifications of upcoming classes and groups.

Jay's personal website, http://www.jayearley.com, contains more of his writings and information about his psychotherapy practice, including his therapy groups.

Our other website, http://www.psychemaps.com, contains a questionnaire to determine which of the seven types of Inner Critics you have and a program to profile your Inner Critic and Inner Champion.

The Online Community (http://www.personal-growth-programs.com/connect) is for people who are reading this book and would like to support each other in letting go of

Perfectionism. It is part of a larger online community of people who are working on their personal growth and healing through our books, websites, and programs.

The Pattern System website, http://thepatternsystem. wikispaces.com, contains an outline of the latest version.

The Center for Self-Leadership is the official IFS organization. Its website, http://www.selfleadership.org, contains IFS articles, trainings, workshops, and a list of IFS therapists.

Books and Booklets by
Jay Earley, PhD and Bonnie Weiss, LCSW

The IFS Series
Self-Therapy (Jay)

Self-Therapy for Your Inner Critic (J&B)

Resolving Inner Conflict (Jay)

Working with Anger in IFS (Jay)

Negotiating for Self-Leadership (Jay)**

The Pattern System Series
Embracing Intimacy (Jay)

Letting Go of Perfectionism (J&B)

Taking Action: Working Through Procrastination
and Achieving Your Goals (Jay)**

A Pleaser No Longer**

The Inner Critic Series
Self-Therapy for Your Inner Critic (J&B)

Illustrated Workbook for Self-Therapy
for Your Inner Critic (Bonnie)

Activating Your Inner Champion
in Place of Your Inner Critic (J&B)

Letting Go of Perfectionism (J&B)

Other Books (Jay)
Interactive Group Therapy

Transforming Human Culture

Inner Journeys

**Forthcoming

Made in the USA
Columbia, SC
07 July 2022